Original title:
Sliding into Winter Like a Pro (Not)

Copyright © 2024 Creative Arts Management OÜ
All rights reserved.

Author: Eleanor Prescott
ISBN HARDBACK: 978-9916-94-180-5
ISBN PAPERBACK: 978-9916-94-181-2

## Careening into the Fifth Season

With boots too big, I take a stride,
My socks are wet, my pants collide.
A patch of ice, I thought was fine,
Now I'm a smiley, dancing pine.

Snowflakes land upon my nose,
I slip again, and how it goes!
The neighbors laugh, it's quite a show,
As I tumble down, a winter pro!

**Falling Flakes and Bouncing Hearts**

The flakes come swirling, what a sight,
I spin in glee, but lose my fight.
A snowman formed of wayward dreams,
Now looks like me, with floppy seams.

I grab my sled, it's time to race,
But alas! I've lost the playful grace.
I coast on by, then crash, oh dear,
With laughter ringing, I face my fear.

## **Inelegant Adventures in the Chill**

Oh look, a hill! I'm feeling bold,
I take a run, but I am sold.
On bumpy bumps, I hope to glide,
But find myself on snowy pride.

My scarf is huge, it wraps my head,
Like a bundled burrito instead.
I tumble down, my arms a-flail,
In winter's grip, I tell the tale.

## Flailing in the Frigid Dance

The icy dance begins tonight,
My feet go left, but body's right.
With mittens on, I wave hello,
To every branch and frosty show.

I waltz with frost, I kick with glee,
I spin and glide, yet can't quite see.
As snowflakes join this wild charade,
I wonder if I'll make the grade.

## **Laughing with Jack Frost**

Cold air bites, we laugh and cheer,
Frosty faces, no winter gear.
Slipping down, we lose our grace,
Chasing snowflakes, a wild race.

Snowball fights turn into blunders,
Laughing loud, through icy thunders.
Giggles echo, no time for frost,
Friendships warm, though socks are tossed.

## Balance Lost in a White Wonderland

Boots a-shuffle, grace in doubt,
One wrong step, a winter pout.
Arms flailing, a comic fall,
Snowmen's giggles, we hear them call.

Sleds go flying, downhill we race,
Landing hard, with snow on our face.
A winter wonder, chaos reigns,
Laughter echoes, our silly gains.

## Unscripted Winter Capers

Winter wild, no script in sight,
Dancing on ice, oh what a fright.
Hats askew, scarves all askance,
Snowy missteps in a frosty dance.

Snow angels flopping, flails and spins,
Finding ourselves in snowy bins.
Chasing laughter, not wintry woes,
Joy in chaos, that's how it goes.

## **Accidental Elegance in the Snow**

Icy pathways, a graceful slide,
Oh no! Watch out for that ride!
Laughter erupts as we tumble down,
Winter's got us, oh what a clown!

Snowflakes spark like a twinkling show,
But falling's the trick we don't quite know.
Wishing for style, but it's pure delight,
In this chill, our hearts feel light.

**The Struggle Begins Anew**

Winter's chill creeps in stealthily,
Pants for snowmen, but I just slip.
Boots on, I'm ready, or so it seems,
Down I go, my plans take a dip.

Cocoa's warmth is my only friend,
Outside, the world is a comic show.
I try to stand, but gravity's keen,
Laughing friends watch my frosty flow.

## **Laughter in the Frost**

I step outside, feeling quite bold,
The ice beneath me says, "Not today!"
My graceful glide turns to a wild roll,
As birds above chirp, 'What a display!'

Snowflakes fall like confetti around,
I tumble and twist, a one-woman show.
Giggles erupt from the shrubs nearby,
While I plot my next move in the snow.

**Falling Leaves and Frosted Dreams**

Leaves are gone, a stark world awaits,
I strategize, it's time to prevail.
Yet one wrong move and, whoops, I am down,
Making snow angels, a winter fail!

The wind plays tricks with my wooly hat,
As I battle with scarves and slippery floors.
Every step's a dance, we laugh and we cry,
Stumbling through dreams, oh winter encore!

# The Art of Icy Entrances

With all my might, I take to the street,
Ice patches lurking, a sneaky foe.
I wave to neighbors, then, oh, what a treat,
A pop and a slide, it's my grand show!

Fenders crunching, laughter ignites,
As I navigate this frozen spree.
Winter's a jester, my clumsy delight,
A slapstick saga, come laugh with me!

## **Sloppy Boots and Drifty Dreams**

My boots are soggy, oh what a sight,
They squelch and they squish, not quite right.
Each step a splatter, a puddle parade,
I laugh at the chaos, it can't be delayed.

With dreams of snowflakes, I take my stance,
I slip on the ice, not just by chance.
A spin and a twirl, I'm a dizzy delight,
In this frosty circus, I dance through the night.

## Frosty Fumbles and Happy Bundles

Bundled in layers, I waddle with glee,
I zip and I wiggle, can't quite be free.
A scarf like a serpent, it drags on the ground,
I trip over laughter, what joy I have found.

Snowballs in hand, we aim for a hit,
But miss and fall down, our fumbles a hit.
Like clowns in a snowstorm, we tumble about,
In frosty fumbles, we laugh and we shout.

## The Wily Ways of Winter's Grip

Winter's not subtle, it's clever and sly,
It tricks me to stumble, oh me oh my!
The sidewalk's a rink, my feet take a spin,
I dance with the frost, my face wearing a grin.

With each little slip, I manage to land,
In a fluffy embrace of the white snowy band.
I chuckle and shake off the frost from my hat,
Winter's a joker, and I'm still the brat.

## **Playful Tumbles on Frozen Stage**

On a stage made of ice, we put on our show,
With slips and with trips, we all steal the flow.
Each pratfall a gem, as we glide and we sway,
Winter's our partner, in this frosty ballet.

With giggles and shouts, we spin with delight,
In this merry mishap, we dance through the night.
Snowflakes are clapping, the audience roars,
For playful tumbles on winter's cold floors.

## Grappling with Gales

The wind whips through with such a howl,
I stumble forth with a clumsy scowl.
My scarf wraps 'round, like a snake in play,
I'm wresting with winter, what a silly fray!

Each gust knocks me to dance in the street,
My feet are flailing, no grace in my beat.
Snowflakes swirl like confetti in air,
Catch me, oh gravity! I'm not prepared!

**Frosted Footsteps**

I step on snow, it glistens and pops,
Then slip on ice, my dignity drops.
A graceful leap turned into a sprawl,
Where's my etiquette? I've none at all!

I walk like a penguin, with wobbly grace,
My hands flail wildly, I'm in a tight race.
The ground feels like glass, beneath my soles,
With every brave step, my confidence rolls!

## Winter's Stumble

A friendly invite to view the snow's glow,
But there I go, slipping headlong in tow.
The laughter erupts as I fumble and fall,
I'm the winter showstopper, I'm having a ball!

With boots that betray at the most crucial times,
I dance like a fool, unwritten in rhymes.
A frosty ballet with no audience near,
But giggles and tumbles fill the chill air!

## The Clutz in the Cold

My mittens are warm, but my grip's in a twist,
A friend takes a snap, oh how could I miss?
Face-first in snow, like a clown out of place,
I rise with a smile, still clutching my grace.

Snowmen are built, but I'm never the pro,
I build a fine mound, topped with wiggle and glow.
With laughter the prize, I embrace my bad falls,
A jester in winter, I'll always enthrall!

## Chill of the Unprepared

The snow starts to fall, oh what a sight,
Bundled up tight, yet feeling no light.
A scarf on my face, a hat on my head,
Tripped on a snowdrift, now I'm seeing red.

My boots are too flashy, they shine like a star,
But the ice on the sidewalk suggests I won't go far.
I dance like a penguin, arms out like a fool,
Wishing I'd learned earlier, what to wear to school.

## A Grapple with Frost

I woke up this morning, what a surprise,
Frost on the window, a chill that pries.
Coffee is brewing, but it feels like snow,
I'll need a warm jacket, I only brought flow.

I step out the door, just to stumble and fall,
It's like I'm auditioning for a comedy haul.
The ground looks so smooth, like a vast shiny sheet,
But underneath awaits a slapstick retreat.

## **Winter's Uninvited Guest**

There's a knock at my door, it's winter, oh dear,
Bringing strange guests, with ice-cold cheer.
Hot cocoa in hand, but it's gone in a blink,
My fingers like icicles, I can barely think.

The car won't start, it's frozen in place,
I'm grappling with frost like it's all just a race.
Chuckling at neighbors in their colorful gear,
I wave with a fumble, my pride full of fear.

**The Slippery Dance of December**

In December's embrace, I try to maintain,
A balance on sidewalks that resemble a train.
Each step feels like salsa, with twirls and some slips,
Hands waving wildly, I'm trying not to trip.

Kids laugh on their sleds, while I battle the snow,
Attempting a stride like a seasoned pro.
But down I go tumbling, with flair and with glee,
Who knew winter's charm would challenge me?

## Bantering with the Chill

Cocoa spills and mismatched socks,
I shuffle out, the frost in blocks.
Winter whispers, 'You're quite the sight,'
I wave back, in my hat too tight.

Snowflakes dance on my handlebar,
I clutch the edges, calling, 'Not far!'
A slip, a slide, the neighbors stare,
I laugh it off, at least I'm here!

**One Foot in Front of the Other, Maybe**

Boots too big, they squeak and squawk,
I take a step, it's more like a walk.
Ice beneath, a treacherous trap,
I wobble like I'm in a slapstick map.

Galloping penguins cheer me on,
As I flail like a ski-less swan.
One foot forward, then two, oh glee!
Winter's no match for my mug of tea!

## **Frosty Feet and Fractured Dreams**

My toes are frozen, dreams on ice,
The slippery walk, not so very nice.
I plot my path, a stealthy pursuit,
But who knew snow could be so... astute?

Each careless step a comedic feat,
I laugh as I dance on frosty feet.
With every tumble, a new cheerleader,
Winter's a jester, and I'm its feeder.

## The Misstep Symphony of Cold

A grand parade of shudders and slips,
Watch my grand performance—no grace, just quips.
I twirl in gusto, my legs all askew,
As if I'm auditioning for 'The Clumsy Crew.'

The music of winter, it plays a tune,
My clattered laughter, a comical boon.
Each misstep a note, each laugh a refrain,
In this frosty ballet, I forget all the pain.

## **Offbeat Waltz of the Wintry Days**

Snowflakes fall like clumsy knickknacks,
I trip on ice, hear my playful cracks.
My scarf flies high, a kite in a gale,
Fumbling about, just like a tale.

Hot cocoa spills down my warm sweater,
With every slip, it can't get better.
Laughter echoes down this slippery lane,
Oops! There goes my dignity—again!

## Jokes on Ice: A Comedy of Errors

Here comes snow just like a prank,
While I slip, the neighbors sang.
Rolled into a pile, I'm quite the sight,
A snowman's laugh fills up the night.

My boots like lead, so hard to steer,
I wave at friends, who disappear.
A tumbler down, I'm on display,
Froze like that, my cheeks all gray.

## **Fumbling Through the Frosty Hours**

The sled's a dream, then a slip and slide,
The kids are laughing, I'll take my pride.
Hot soup I spill, a saucy affair,
Too much pepper brings out my glare.

My hat's a gift from a cat, I swear,
With every bounce, I'm gasping for air.
Chasing my mittens, lost in a ditch,
Oh winter, you've turned me into a witch!

## Winter's Tumbleweeds of Laughter

Tumbleweeds of snow roll down the street,
I trip, I roll, now aren't I neat?
A flurry of giggles follows my fall,
Just a winter fool, having a ball.

Mittens tangled in my coat's tight hug,
Try to stand tall, but I'm stuck like a bug.
My friends can't help but to jeer and tease,
Oh, what a sight, this winter, please!

## Whimsical Whirls of Icy Air

The frosty wind catches my hat,
As I tumble like an awkward cat.
Slipping on ice, I spread my wings,
Facing the world and all its zings.

Snowflakes dance as I lose my grip,
My boots do a quick and quirky slip.
Giggles escape from onlookers near,
Who knew winter could bring such cheer?

A holiday wreath hangs askew,
While I attempt to make my debut.
With arms flailing like a windmill's spin,
Finding my laughter beneath this din.

Oh, the joy in this chilly plight!
As I embrace each frosty bite.
With each stumble, my spirits rise,
In this whimsical whirl of surprise!

## Laughing Off the Frostbitten Failures

Footprints scattered like a jigsaw puzzle,
Each step forward brings a new huzzle.
I laugh aloud as I lose the race,
Frostbitten fingers and a rosy face.

My snowman leans like he's had a drink,
A crooked smile, oh how I think!
Gloves too big, and a scarf too long,
Yet somehow I sing my winter song.

Neighbors giggle from their warm abodes,
Watching me tumble and roll down roads.
Hot cocoa later will bring me cheer,
After my antics, it's finally here!

But every fall is a story told,
Of winter fun and laughter bold.
In this frosty carnival of fails,
I twirl and spin with icy trails.

## **Stumbling Toward the Sparkle of Snow**

Chasing glimmers as they catch my eye,
With every step, it's a comical try.
A trip and a tumble, oh what a show,
In pursuit of the sparkle that glimmers below.

My boots betray me in the soft, white fluff,
Each effort to march is a haphazard bluff.
With arms wide open, I dive in delight,
Rolling in crystals under moonlight bright.

A snowball flies – oh, here comes the aim,
But alas! My face is the target of fame.
Laughter erupts, from friends all around,
In this frosty circus, winter's famed ground.

Yet onward I waddle, with grace gone astray,
Toward glittering wonders at the end of the day.
Through snowflakes and giggles, my heart is aglow,
As I stumble and bounce toward the winter's show.

## Chasing Shadows in the Chill

The world turns white as I step outside,
With big dreams of grace, but my balance has lied.
I leap into shadows that flicker and dance,
Only to land in a slippery trance.

Snow pants crinkle with a flimsy sound,
As I wiggle and squirm on the glistening ground.
Laughter cascades like a soft winter breeze,
While a snowball ambush brings me to my knees.

Ski poles waving as I glide with finesse,
Only to trip – oh, sweet winter mess!
But who cares about elegance in this spree,
When fun is the goal, so wild and so free.

Each tumble a tale, I greet the cold air,
In this playful chase, I have not a care.
So here's to the winter, with chuckles and thrills,
In a world of white, where laughter fulfills.

## Sledding on the Edge of Grace

In boots too big, I start my run,
With laughter loud, I think it's fun.
The hill looks steep, the snow's so bright,
I tuck my chin, and brace for flight.

A whoosh, a thud, a splendid fall,
I land like jelly; is that a sprawl?
My sled is stuck, I'm on my back,
A glorious mess, a snowball hack.

The icy breeze, it bites my nose,
With cheeks like apples, I strike a pose.
Each tumble's laughter, a wintry cheer,
But please, no photos, let's keep this clear!

Amidst the giggles from the crowd,
I wave my hands, feeling proud.
For every slip, there's fun to gain,
I'll rise again, and do it all again!

## A Slip and a Slide Through Time's Shift

A puffer coat, it weighs a ton,
I waddle forth, prepared for fun.
But as I plant my sturdy foot,
My balance flops, I come unglued.

With arms flailing like a bird,
I slip and slide, it's quite absurd.
The snowflakes laugh as I take a dive,
In my frosty dance, I feel alive.

Through icy patches, I try to steer,
With every step, I face my fear.
An epic journey through winter's tease,
Each misstep brings me to my knees.

But look! I'm laughing, joy on replay,
Who needs control on this wild display?
Let's skate through life, take every slip,
For every crash, there's a joyful trip!

**Unexpected Thuds of Frosty Delight**

The snowflakes swirl, they mock my grace,
I bound outside, a bright red face.
But one wrong step, oh what a sight,
I plummet down, like a beaver's bite.

A friendly tree saves me from doom,
With branches hugging, it clears my gloom.
I'm camouflaged in the snowy white,
Wishing for warmth and a cozy night.

With friends, we gather, a frosty cheer,
They tell the tales I prefer not here.
But laughter chimes in winter's sound,
As I try to stand, I'm flat on the ground.

Oh joy is found in every fall,
With winter's chill, we can't stand tall.
So here's to slips and frosty play,
Each thud brings smiles to light our way!

**Navigating the Icebound Uncertainty**

With a map of snow, I plot my course,
But every footstep feels like a force.
The world's a blur, a frozen maze,
I spin around in an icy daze.

I reach for trees; they just laugh back,
Their frozen limbs, they hide the track.
An ice patch looms, I chance the glide,
A slip and a spin, oh where's my pride?

The laughter echoes, winter's choir,
As I tango with nature, slipping prior.
Like penguins chic, we waddle here,
Each twist and turn invokes a cheer.

But with each fall, I'm meeting fate,
Navigating chaos can't be too late.
For in this play, we dance and collide,
Winter's embrace, our joy-filled ride!

## **Mirth and Mischief in the Chill**

Snowflakes land on my nose,
A wobbly stand, oh how it goes!
With laughter bursting from my lips,
I tumble down on frosty trips.

Hot cocoa in my eager hands,
With marshmallows like fluffy bands.
I spill it all with a big cheer,
And sip again while shedding a tear.

The sled won't steer, it's all a game,
I zigzag wildly, I'm not to blame!
Winter's magic makes me grin,
As I dive belly-first, let the fun begin!

Oh, what a sight, a jolly fall,
Snow-capped glee, I'm having a ball.
With every slip, my joy returns,
In this chilly dance, my spirit burns.

## **Clumsy Steps on Crystal Paths**

Wandering on this icy floor,
Who knew 'footwear' was a lore?
Each step's a gamble, oh so slick,
I'm like a puppet on a stick.

A graceful twirl turns into flops,
With every stomp, my balance hops.
I wave at friends, but slip and slide,
Laughter erupts, no place to hide.

Beneath the moon, my feet take flight,
But gravity's pulling, try as I might.
A comical crash, an epic fail,
Yet warm-hearted chuckles prevail.

Oh winter, you've got a sense of fun,
Even when my feet are on the run.
I stumble and roll, I'll embrace the freeze,
In this frosty chaos, I feel so free!

## The Dance of Frosty Feet

To shimmy and shake on frost-kissed ground,
I feel like a star, 'til I lose my crown.
A twirl, a spin, then oops, I fall,
Nature's happy stage, a comedy hall.

With laughter ringing through the air,
My graceful moves turn into a scare.
Legs tangled up in a frosty art,
Winter pranks playing on my heart.

Boots lost their grip, what a surprise,
As I surf through snow, my feet start to fly.
Pine trees giggle, the snowballs gleam,
Each misstep fuels my winter dream.

With flailing arms, I seize the chance,
In awkward motions, I find my dance.
A jig of joy, I can't deny,
Unless I land on the ground—oh my!

# Graceful Escapes from Autumn's Grasp

Falling leaves in a crispy whirl,
'Twas autumn's farewell, my toes twirl.
But here comes winter with sly delight,
Time to tackle this frosty fight.

I leap through puddles, icy and bright,
A glistening surface becomes my plight.
With each hop, I miss the mark,
Landing in snow, it's a snowy park!

Jackets puffy, like marshmallows piled,
In my winter gear, I'm like a wild child.
With hats askew and scarves that snake,
I tumble around for fun's sweet sake.

The sun begins to dip down low,
But laughter rings as I put on a show.
With every slip, I dance between joy,
These frosty moments, oh winter's ploy!

## **Each Fall a Story Untold**

Leaves cascade like laughter loud,
A crisp reminder, winter's shroud.
With every step, a comical plight,
As gravity plays a sneaky bite.

Scarf wrapped tight, I take a chance,
Feet in skids, I try to dance.
Each tumble tells a tale anew,
Like a clumsy deer in morning dew.

Snowball fights get wildly serious,
My aim could make the stoutest curious.
With every slip, I share a grin,
Nature's prankster buried within.

Yet each mishap, a badge of glee,
Proving winter's a playful spree.
From frost-bitten toes to laughter loud,
Each fall returns me to the crowd.

## Grace Gone Awry in the Snow

With dreams of ballet, I hit the road,
A pirouette turns into a code.
Flailing arms, my balance betrays,
This wintry stage that twists my ways.

Trying to twirl but fate has a laugh,
A slip and a slide, now you do the math.
Spinning in circles, I'm lost in a swirl,
Behold my artistry's ungraceful whirl.

Snowflakes glisten, oh such a tease,
While I face-plant, with effortless ease.
A grand display of elegance spurned,
With every flop, my dignity burned.

Still I waddle, my spirit won't fade,
A misguided ballet, my own charade.
For in the chaos, a dancer's heart,
Even when winter plays its part.

## Timid Steps on the Slippery Path

In boots that waddle like a duck,
I tread the path with little luck.
Each hesitant move, a careful joke,
As my confidence begins to choke.

A patch of ice, a glimmer unseen,
My pirouette, oh so unclean!
The ground's a joker, and I'm its fool,
In this wintry game, I'm nobody's tool.

Glances shared, laughter ignites,
Onlookers witness my comical flights.
A hesitant shuffle, I cling to the rail,
As a snowman watches, but feels no frail.

Yet through the giggles and cautious fright,
I find the joy in this frosty bite.
For life's a dance with rhythmic unknowns,
In timid steps, my laughter homes.

## Daring to Tread Where Angels Fear

With bravado fueled by hot cocoa bliss,
I leap into winter, a snow-covered kiss.
Yet beneath my bravado, shadows conspire,
As I dance with disaster, I surely retire.

A corner too sharp, my bravest of yelps,
Whirlwinds of snow tease my clumsy help.
In this frosty arena, jokes of despair,
Angels would giggle, yet I fight the air.

Each step too bold, each move too grand,
Feathered flakes greet me, a slippery hand.
What was a stride now becomes a slide,
Waves of laughter, as I clash and collide.

Yet here I stumble, dauntless and free,
'Cause the world is a stage, and I'm meant to be.
With angels above, and magic below,
I embrace every falter, revel in the show.

## Bumbling Through the Flakes

With frosty breath and wayward feet,
I stumble forth in winter's greet.
Snowflakes dance like little jesters,
My balance fails, it's quite the festers.

A mitten slips, my scarf's a mess,
Caught in a snowball, I confess.
Laughter echoes from my plight,
As I assess my snowy fight.

## The Comedy of Winter's Embrace

I gear up snug, then out I go,
In dreams of grace, but oh, the woe!
A patch of ice, a flailing yelp,
I land with flair, no sign of help.

Sleds should glide, yet mine's a brick,
It flies too fast, it's not a trick.
My friends all laugh, I nod along,
In this spectacle, I belong.

## **Winter's Uninvited Guests**

Snowmen rise with hats askew,
While I trip over things I flew.
A squirrel steals my snacks with glee,
As I watch, yelling, "Hey! That's me!"

Pine needles scratch, my nose turns red,
From hot cocoa spills, I'd rather dread.
Their winter shindig brings new pals,
My inner self, it just befouls.

**Stumbling into Snowy Surprises**

Each step I take feels like a dance,
Yet every slip, I lose my chance.
A snowbank calls, I heed its cry,
Down I tumble, oh me, oh my!

My boots are wet, my socks are cold,
Adventures come, but they feel old.
With laughter bright, I greet the chill,
In this chaos, I find my will.

## The Clumsiness of Chilling Nights

Frosty breath as I step outside,
Socks too thick, I'm like an ice slide.
A snowflake lands just on my nose,
And down I go, in frozen pose.

Laughter echoes through the cold air,
As I tumble without a care.
A sled dog's smirk as I fall flat,
My dignity lost, just like that!

Fingers numb, but I can't feel shame,
Fumbling 'round like it's a game.
Snowman grins with a frosty cheer,
While I just hope my friends stay near.

In the evening light, things get bright,
With fuzzy mittens, I slip mid-flight.
The chattering teeth, the soft white ground,
I frolic like a goofy hound.

## **Tripping Over Tomorrow's Sled**

Tomorrow's plans with snow in tow,
But here I am, moving slow.
Tripping over a pile of fluff,
This graceful dance is quite enough!

Bouncing hopes on a slickened street,
With each step, I admit defeat.
A sled that waits in the frosty gloom,
As I tumble headfirst into a broom.

Laughter rolls from the starry skies,
While I pick snowflakes from my eyes.
Falling soft like a winter duck,
It's all in good jest, good luck!

Every slip just adds more glee,
Tomorrow's snowman laughs at me.
With giggles shared, we're in this mess,
A joyful tangle, I must confess.

## **Mischievous Whispers of Cold**


A crisp chill wraps around my frame,
The wind's a tease, it knows my name.
Sneaky gusts pull me down with glee,
In my frosty dance, where's the tea?

Snowflakes dance and swirl about,
While I stumble, laugh, and shout.
Clever ice leads me on a spree,
I land in snow, giggling with glee.

Chilly whispers, they call my name,
Each misstep feels like a game.
Falling snow hides my every bruise,
As I promise to never refuse.

With every try, a face-plant score,
The ground below, it begs for more.
Yet in this freeze, joy takes its hold,
In winter's embrace, I dare be bold.

## Staggering into the Solstice

As winter approaches, wobbly and spry,
With boots too big, I aim for the sky.
Navigating paths like a drunken knight,
My plans collapse with each featured fright.

Tonight's the night for laughter and light,
But first, I tumble—now that's a sight!
Snowballs thrown in the name of fun,
While I'm buried deep, just another one.

Frosty cheeks and a merry jig,
Twisting around, I feel quite big.
Twirling wide, I forget cold's sting,
Each little flop starts my heart to sing.

Through the evening's whims, I will sway,
With laughter filling the night's ballet.
Though clumsy, I'm here to stake my claim,
Celebrating winter, I'll take the blame.

## A Tangle of Wool and Frost

Hats askew and socks mismatched,
A scarf wraps tight, a face attached.
The icy air, it nips and bites,
Clumsy steps on frosty nights.

My mitten flops, it's lost the fight,
A dance on ice, what a delight!
With every slip, I try to trot,
Falling hard, but laughing a lot.

The snowmen stare with icy grins,
As I perform my graceful spins.
My coat too big, I waddle wide,
A wooly paunch, I cannot hide.

So here's to those who trip and slide,
With friends nearby, we'll laugh with pride.
Let winter come with frosty flair,
For tangled wool, it's all to share.

## Frosty Footfalls and Whimsical Missteps

With frosted ground, I take my stand,
But oh, my feet have their own plan.
The crunch of snow—a quiet dare,
Each step a gamble, do I care?

A leap! A twist! A cheerful yell,
I pirouette, then straight to hell.
My neighbors laugh and cheer aloud,
As I perform for the wintry crowd.

Gloves like bricks, they grip so tight,
Wobbling on this slippery sight.
A tumble here, a roll or two,
Who knew this cold could harbor goo?

But joy arises in those falls,
The giggles echo through these halls.
So let the snow bring happy spills,
In winter's laugh, we find our thrills.

## **Navigating the Glacial Clownery**

Stepping out, I make my way,
Where icy patches seem to play.
With every step, a jolly slip,
My friends all rolling, can't find grip.

The frosty air, it bites my nose,
As I leap like a clumsy prose.
With every fall, I give a grin,
This frosty fun, I'll surely win.

Boots like anchors, heavy and slow,
I march like a penguin in a show.
A frosty twist, then down I go,
The snow is soft—what a magical blow!

It's all a game, this slippery jest,
With laughter bubbling in my chest.
So take my hand, let's make a mess,
In this glacial clownery, we are blessed.

## Joyous Stumbles in the Winter Light

Winter whispers, soft and bright,
While I tumble into the night.
My feet, they dance, away they go,
How many times? I've lost count, though.

With cheeks like apples, red and round,
I trip on paths of frozen ground.
The laughter echoes through the air,
As I practice my winter flair.

Mittens fly and scarves unwind,
Falling gracefully, I don't mind.
Each bit of snow, a cushion made,
For joyful stumbles, I'm not afraid.

So raise a mug, let's toast the cold,
To frosty fun and tales retold.
In every slip, there's pure delight,
In joyous stumbles, we find our light.

## **Frosty Missteps**

The snowflakes fall like little bows,
I step outside, and down I goes.
With flailing arms, I try to stand,
A dance of winter not quite planned.

My hat's askew, the cold bites deep,
A snowball lands, it's just too steep.
While others glide with grace so fine,
I'm just a penguin drawing a line.

With laughter ringing all around,
I take my tumble on the ground.
A frosty laugh, a frigid cheer,
Oh winter, you've got me here!

But as I shiver, I still declare,
This winter's fun, beyond compare.
With every slip, a story grows,
A winter tale that everyone knows.

## Clumsy in the Cold

Dressed in layers, I hit the street,
My boots are new, but still, I cheat.
An icy patch, a sudden jerk,
A graceful glide? More like a quirk.

Snowflakes tumble, a frosty dance,
I trip over my own advance.
The world spins 'round, I twist and twirl,
Oh, this winter's giving a whirl!

Friends are laughing, I join the show,
In winter's waltz, I'm just a no-show.
With every slip, a giggle shared,
It's all in fun, though somewhat scared.

Yet still I rise to face the day,
With chilly cheeks, I'll find my way.
In this clumsiness, I see the cheer,
Winter's mischief, we hold so dear.

# A Winter's Wobble

I venture out with a brave face,
But soon my feet lose all their grace.
A slip, a trip, I feel the rush,
A winter's wobble, oh what a hush!

Snowballs fly as laughter sings,
I can't tell if it's joy or flings.
My gloves are wet, my heart's alight,
This chilly scene feels just so right.

Each tumble's met with merry cheer,
I laugh away the slip and smear.
With friends beside, we're all a mess,
Embracing every frosty guess.

Yet here I stand, a jumbled sight,
In winter's chill, I find my light.
With every wobble, with every fall,
We just have fun, and that's the call.

## **Icicles and Inexperience**

With icicles hanging like spears bright,
I step outside, ready to fight.
But as I turn, my foot's too slow,
And down I go, headfirst in snow!

My scarf's a knot, my boots untied,
I laugh aloud, I can't have pride.
While others glide on winter's stage,
I'm but a fool trapped in a cage.

But joy is found in each failed grace,
In each mistake, a smiling face.
With icicles glistening in the sun,
I know this winter's meant for fun.

So here I stand, both proud and cold,
With tales of slips and spills retold.
Inexperience makes winter bright,
With every laugh, we find delight.

## Naivety of Snowflakes

With dreams of snowflakes swirling down,
I donned my boots of yellow brown.
But slipped and flopped with playful grace,
I landed in a frosty embrace.

The kids around in laughter rolled,
While I just knew I'd soon be cold.
I thought I'd build a snowman tall,
Instead, a pile, trampoline fall.

Snowball fights were meant for me,
But missed my target, oh, direto!
I launched a flurry, hit my neighbor,
Who smiled and hugged the caper labor.

So now I sit on my hot cocoa,
Wishing winter was a big no-no.
With silly tales of snowy spree,
I laugh at my snowy folly, whee!

## The Frosty Faux Pas

Bundled up like a polar bear,
I stepped outside without a care.
But as I strutted, turned to greet,
I slipped upon a patch of sleet.

My hat flew off, my scarf unspooled,
The neighbors laughed, I felt like a fool.
I tried to waltz, but failed in stride,
The sidewalk's edge was far too wide.

Attempted snowmen turned out lean,
A wobbly thing, no king or queen.
I crowned it with a crisp old sock,
Declared it art, the laughing stock.

So if you see me out and about,
In winter gear, don't scream or shout.
Just know that underneath the flair,
Is someone prone to frosty despair.

# A Dance with Frostbite

In the winter chill, my boots did slide,
I spun around with arms open wide.
A graceful move turned to a tumble,
As laughter erupted, my pride did crumble.

I twirled with joy, but alas too fast,
And found my dignity in the past.
With cheeks aglow, we danced in snow,
While I'd much prefer a warm salsa show.

The ice beneath became my stage,
As I crafted a clumsy winter page.
Every twist and every spin,
Led to giggles hidden within my grin.

So, here's my toast to winter's glee,
To every slip, a memory!
Though frostbite may chill my jolly-core,
I'll dance again, I swear, once more!

## Ungraceful Greetings to the Dark Season

As autumn bids its sweet adieu,
I waved to winter, oh so new.
But slippery paths got in the way,
And down I went, what a display!

With arms flailing like a windmill grand,
My dignity slipped right from my hand.
The snowflakes chuckled, the trees did sway,
While I faced the ground in pure dismay.

Each frosty breath a comic jest,
In boots two sizes too big, no less.
A tumble here, a tumble there,
Who knew winter would not be fair?

So cheers to all the oops and slips,
To winter's joy that often trips.
I'll greet the season with a grin,
For laughter's warmth, that's how we win!

## Dance of the Uncoordinated

I stepped outside, my feet took flight,
A dance with ice, oh what a sight.
With one grand twirl, down I did go,
Performing a slip, my limbs all aglow.

The dog laughed loud, as I embraced the ground,
My dignity lost, without a sound.
Attempting ballet on an icy stage,
Turns out I'm better at flipping with rage!

Snowflakes giggle in their frosty play,
While I fumble and fall in a zany display.
A pirouette gone wrong, a glide gone bad,
The winter's my foe, but I'm not too sad.

So here I am, in my winter wear,
An unchoreographed show, too funny to bear.
The frosty stage calls me back for a round,
As I shuffle and tumble, my joy knows no bound.

## **Winter's Joyful Misadventures**

Grabbed my scarf, stepped out for fun,
But a gust of wind said, 'Not just one!'
I swayed like a tree, caught in the breeze,
While snowflakes danced, asking for ease.

My boots betrayed me, what a disgrace,
They're more like skates in this icy race.
With a grin and a laugh, I took to the street,
A frosty adventure, could it be beat?

Children throw snowballs, a game full of cheer,
While I trip on a mound and disappear.
A snow angel formed -- not the one I planned,
Just flailing and flopping like a fish on land.

So let's raise a toast to the slips and the falls,
To wintertime chaos, the laughter that calls.
With a hot cocoa, we'll sit by the fire,
And reminisce about how we just can't inspire!

## **The Clumsy Snowfall Symphony**

As it starts to snow, I step out in style,
An orchestra of slips, all cheerful and guile.
Each note of my stumble a melody sweet,
In the symphony of winter, I dance on my feet.

The flakes come swirling, a ballet of white,
While I compose chaos with all of my might.
A double spin twist, oops! Down I go,
An audience of squirrels, their giggles do flow.

My mittens are fuzzy, my hat's askew,
It's an artful disaster, a clumsy debut.
With each snowy plummet, my joy takes the lead,
As I twirl through the drifts in a frosty stampede.

So let's all join, and play in this rush,
In the "Chocolate" ballroom, there's never a hush.
The music of laughter, the rhythm of fun,
In this clumsy waltz, we're all number one!

# Unprepared for the Chill

Bundled up tight, I stepped through the door,
Expecting a blast, but got hit by a roar.
The wind got my hair, made it stand up tall,
While I tried to grab hold of nothing at all.

With a skip and a shuffle, I thought I'd glide,
But the ice had plans, it took me for a ride.
A face full of snow, I emerged with a grin,
"Who knew winter's Narnia would let me dive in?"

My hot cocoa's cold, with marshmallows gone,
While the snowmen chuckle, they think I'm a con.
A virtue in falling, who knew it could be,
The secret to joy in this icy spree?

So here's my farewell to the chill in the air,
With laughter and warmth, nothing can compare.
Forget about grace, let's embrace the fun,
The frosty mischief, it's just begun!

## Cold Comfort and Awkward Moments

Falling down is quite a feat,
In winter boots that just can't compete.
Snowflakes land on noses bright,
Laughter follows every clumsy flight.

Sipping cocoa, I trip on a mat,
Spilling warmth, how about that?
Slippers slide like socks on ice,
Who knew winter would be so nice?

Mittens tangled, looking like a fool,
Stumbling over that one ice jewel.
But hey, a giggle's worth the cold,
In awkward moments, warmth unfolds.

So bring on the snowballs for a fight,
Embrace the fumbles with all your might.
With jokes and jests, our cheer won't freeze,
In these winter antics, we find our ease.

## **Winter's Clumsy Masquerade**

Oh, I donned my coat with flair,
Only to trip on my own glare.
Dark clouds laugh in snowy jest,
As I tumble, the world's a fest.

Frosty breath and wobbly steps,
Skating gracefully? Nah, just missteps.
Snowflakes swirl like little ghosts,
While I chase them, I'll surely roast.

Balloons of laughter fill the air,
As I slip and slide without a care.
The snowman grins, what a sight,
Don't take it serious, it's all delight!

With scarves askew and hats amiss,
Winter's charm is not to dismiss.
As we dance through the flurries so bold,
In this clumsy masquerade, joy is gold.

## Laughter Echoing Through Snow-Dusted Trees

Amidst the pines, a sound rings free,
It's laughter dancing through the trees.
A tumble here, a slip there too,
Nature chuckles with every view.

Snowflakes tease, landing on heads,
While I'm busy trying to shed,
The layers of clothes that make me round,
It's a fashion show on frozen ground!

Each misstep echoes, a silly song,
Winter antics can't be wrong.
The trusty sled takes off with a cheer,
Turns into a rocket, oh dear, oh dear!

So here we roll in winter's praise,
With giggles bright as the sun's warm rays.
Every stumble a tale to tell,
In this snowy land, we all know well.

## The Sway of Sleds and Slips

Gather 'round for sledding thrills,
But hold on tight, it's full of spills!
Round and round, we wobble along,
Sleds take flight with a joyous song.

Launching off, I take to the hill,
Hoping this ride gives me a chill.
But wait, what's that? A hidden lump,
A veer to the left, oh what a thump!

Wipeouts happen, it's part of the game,
Snow angels made from sledding fame.
Laughter erupts in frosty air,
As we tumble, no worry, no care.

With cheeks all red and spirits high,
Winter's magic we can't deny.
As we glide and slip with delight,
Each moment a joy, each fall feels right.

## **Winter's Icy Trials**

As I step outside, it feels like a slide,
My boots are betrayed, what a snowy glide!
I wobble and wobble, try to keep my grace,
But the ice has a laugh, a smirk on my face.

Hot cocoa in hand, I brave the cold air,
But with every sip, my gloves start to tear.
A snowball approaches, oh what a face!
A wintery duel? More like a slip race.

The shovel waits, like a mischievous friend,
I dig and I push, but the fun won't end.
Each scoop turns to chaos, a comedy show,
As the snowflakes dance, and my patience runs low.

So here's to the season of frosty delight,
Where each step I take, I'm ready for flight!
With laughter and falls, it's the best kind of cheer,
Embracing the chill, let the fun disappear!

# **Tripping Through the Frost**

The ground turns to marble, my feet start to float,
I'm a graceful ballerina, till I hit a snow moat!
With a flail and a splash, I'm lost in the scene,
A spectacle guaranteed, like a slapstick routine.

Snowflakes surround, they dance down my coat,
A scarf wrapped so tight, I can hardly gloat.
I try to look cool, like I know what I'm doing,
But my socks are now soggy; I feel them a-stewing.

A waltz with my dog, but it turns into mud,
We're tapping the rhythm of a wintery flood.
With one little trip, chaos starts to ensue,
The snowman just giggles, what else can he do?

So I'll grin through the falls and wear that bright hat,
When winter arrives, who cares about that?
For laughter's the key in this frosty parade,
Let the cold winds whirl, I'll still be well-played!

## A Comedic Chill

I donned my warm gear, feeling quite fine,
But it turns out my jacket is three sizes benign.
Zipping it up feels like a bear in a chair,
If I move too quick, oh my, beware!

The ski slopes are gleaming, I'm ready to soar,
But my skills on the board? They slam to the floor.
With a twist and a turn, I view my defeat,
As I tumble and roll, winter's dojo of heat.

A hot drink in hand, I'm a king for a while,
But just one little slip, and I'm lost in a pile.
With my face in the snow, I'm a sight to behold,
A frosty endeavor, the legend retold.

So here's to the chill, with its fall and its glee,
When winter comes laughing, let it come for me!
With friends all around, we'll share in the jest,
Let the winter winds blow; we'll always be blessed!

## **Awkward Embrace of the Flurries**

The flakes softly fall like a clumsy ballet,
My arms windmill wildly, they just want to play.
One misstep is all it takes for a flop,
And soon I'm a snowman, no way to stop!

With mittens that slip, the snowballs they fly,
My aim is quite poor, oh well, say goodbye!
I wave to a friend, but the wind steals the spark,
And my hair turns to icicles — what a wild lark!

Sliding on paths like I'm part of a show,
"Look at me now!" falls a hundred below.
The squirrels just chuckle, they're dancing so spry,
While I do the splits, in defeat I comply.

Yet, laughter is warming beneath all the frost,
In this chaotic cheer, nobody's lost.
When winter comes knocking, embrace the delight,
For the fun comes alive in the cold of the night!

## **Frolics and Falls in the Frost**

The snowflakes dance, I lose my feet,
A graceful tumble, oh what a feat.
I meant to leap, but down I go,
My dignity, resting in the snow.

A winter wonder, yet tripping is real,
Chasing my dog, oh how I squeal!
He runs with glee, as I lose my balance,
Nature's own comedic, icy malice.

With mittens warm, I overreach,
A spin, a flop, then I try to teach.
Just one more step, I'll surely glide,
Instead, I end up in a snowbank wide!

Laughter echoes, a chorus of clatter,
Frolics and falls, what could be better?
Through frosty grass and icy mire,
We all slip some, but we'll never tire!

## A Slip on the Icy Path of Life

With every step, I feel so bold,
But watch me slip, the story's told.
A laugh erupts, the ground is slick,
I'm drafting plays for a slapstick flick.

A shuffle here, a shimmy there,
I'm battling ice like one would dare.
My feet are flyin', oh what a sight,
A ballet dance gone wrong tonight.

The ground is cold, my cheeks are red,
I can't help giggling—whoops! I said.
Life's little slips, we all have those,
But in winter's grip, humor grows.

Each frosty step, a bridge to cross,
From fumble and frown to a hearty toss.
With snowflakes swirling, I take my chance,
To laugh daily, winter's own dance!

**Falling for the Frigid Months**

Oh winter chill, you're quite the tease,
I venture out in my best of ease.
A confident strut, gives way to woe,
Feet fly astray in the white-gloved show.

Around the corner, a patch of ice,
I do a flip, unexpected and nice.
The neighbors chuckled, oh what a scene,
My acrobatic flair, a frosty dream.

An orchestrated slip, oh take a bow,
Watch me tumble, don't ask me how.
I'll write a book on how to fall,
And learn to cherish a winter ball!

Through flurries and giggles, I stand so bold,
Each frosty mishap, a memory told.
For we're all a bit clumsy, it's plain to see,
In the grasp of winter, we'll laugh with glee!

## **Awkward Twirls in the Snow**

Spinning round, I lose my track,
An awkward twirl leaves me with a whack.
I'm channeling grace, but that's a jest,
As I crash softly, bundled up best.

The snowy stage, my frosty friend,
Round and round, where does it end?
My hat flies off, into a drift,
The wind joins in on this comic gift.

Fallen leaves are now white and pure,
But my balance, a riddle, unsure.
Each slip and slide, a laugh in store,
As I tumble forth, I shout for more!

Across the field, we spin and sway,
Winter's here in a playful display.
Amidst the cold, we let out a cheer,
Awkward twirls bring us warmth and cheer!

## Winter's Laughter Catches Us Off Guard

The snowflakes twirl with glee,
But I trip on my own two feet.
A sledge of giggles fills the air,
As I land on my backside, unaware.

Hot cocoa spills, the mug takes flight,
An ice rink forms with just one bite.
I wave to friends as I topple down,
In snowy splendor, I'm the clown.

Woolen hats won't keep me warm,
As I frolic in this frosty storm.
My mittens dance like falling leaves,
While laughter echoes through the eaves.

Yet in this chill, I find delight,
With every mishap, I take flight.
Through winter's grasp, I twirl and spin,
As joy erupts from within!

## **Stumbles in the Snowy Dance**

The world, a canvas draped in white,
I attempt a waltz, but it's a fright.
With arms outstretched, I take my cue,
And promptly fall as if it's new.

A tumble here, a slip right there,
I'm a comedy of snowy despair.
Snowmen roared at my tangled feet,
As I pirouette, their laughter's sweet.

No rhythm found in frozen air,
I land in piles, without a care.
Each step, a risk of frosty fumbles,
Where even the snowflakes giggle and grumble.

Still, I rise with a heart so bold,
In this snowy tale, let joy unfold.
A dance of mishaps, warm and bright,
In winter's grip, I find my light!

## **Elegant Avoidance of Frostbite Follies**

A scarf wrapped tight, my fashion's on show,
Yet I forget how slippery paths glow.
With each step forward, I lose my grace,
As frostbites retreat, I quicken my pace.

Stomping through drifts, mischief awaits,
And frosty paws can't cover my fate.
With elegance lacking, I slide round and round,
In a comedic ballet where cold is renowned.

A dance with the icicles, oh what a sight,
As cold fingers wave, I take to flight.
Yet warmth feels near; I'll laugh through it all,
With frostbite avoided, I give winter a call!

So here's to the slips and the unexpected play,
Where elegance crumbles, and laughter holds sway.
With a wink and a shuffle, the game is on,
In winter's embrace, I dance till dawn!

## **Slippery Seasons and Wobbly Souls**

The frosty wind sings a wobbly tune,
While I try to walk like a graceful loone.
But one step forward leads to two back,
As whimsy whirls in this comical track.

My boots like ice skates, they slip and slide,
As I venture forth with a wintery pride.
"Look! A snow angel," I shout with a grin,
While each tumble brings hearty laughter within.

With every spin, I make my mark,
As laughter ignites in the chilly park.
Oh, to embrace the slippery seas,
And know that joy can be found in these freeze!

So come join the dance in this frosty whirl,
Where fun is afoot and snowflakes twirl.
In winter's hold, we shall make our way,
With wobbly souls on this bright, snowy day!

Milton Keynes UK
Ingram Content Group UK Ltd.
UKHW021350011224
451618UK00023B/238